4

MATTHEW

Why a Messiah?

By Greg Rommel

CPH

SAINT LOUIS

Edited by Thomas A. Nummela

Rachel C. Hoyer, editorial associate

We solicit your comments and suggestions concerning this material. Please write to Product Manager, Youth Bible Studies, Concordia Publishing House, 3558 S. Jefferson Avenue, St. Louis, MO 63118-3968.

Scripture quotations taken from the HOLY BIBLE, NEW INTERNATIONAL VERSION®. NIV®. Copyright © 1973, 1978, 1984 by International Bible Society. Used by permission of Zondervan Publishing House. All rights reserved.

1   2   3   4   5   6   7   8   9   10   05   04   03   02   01   00   99   98   97   96

Contents

BOWOOD GOSPEL CHAPEL

Welcome to *Bible Insights!*

Welcome to the *Bible Insights* series of Bible studies for youth! These materials are designed to provide study opportunities that explore selected books of the Bible in depth and apply the wisdom these books impart to the real-life issues young people face. Each book in this series has been carefully prepared to speak to the needs and concerns of youth, providing insight from God's Word. Each book consists of four sessions of study and can be used for weekly group Bible study, individual study, or a Bible-study retreat or seminar.

This book is designed for the leader of the sessions. It provides all the information and instructions necessary for an effective Bible study. Each study includes material you can reproduce for the students in your group. Additional information on the Bible book to be studied and some helpful information about small-group Bible studies are included in the Introduction.

May God bless your study by the Spirit's power, as you lead young people to greater insight about God's Word and the good things God desires to bring through it to their lives.

Introduction
to the Book of Matthew

Purpose and Theme

For thousands of years, the people of God had anticipated the coming of the Messiah, God's promised Savior King. This four-session course explores the fulfillment of these promises in Jesus. Only the heavenly Father could provide the one necessary for the redemption of His people. God was reconciling the world to Himself! As we search the Gospel of Matthew we will see how Jesus was the One whom God sent with authority and power to be the Messiah.

The Gospel of Matthew

Matthew (also called Levi) was a Jew, a tax collector who left his work to follow Jesus. He wrote his account of our Lord's life and ministry sometime between 55 and 75 A.D. The theme of Matthew's gospel is the proclamation of the messianic King who fulfilled the Old Testament promises to God's people. To prove to Jewish readers that Jesus is the Messiah, Matthew writes about Christ's authority to teach, power to heal, and His suffering, death, and resurrection from the dead.

Some would say that Matthew relied on Mark's gospel for information. More important, Matthew's gospel both agrees with and supplements Mark's. There are many stories in Matthew that are not found elsewhere, such as the visit to Bethlehem of the Wise Men from the east, the flight to Egypt, and the healing of two blind men. Also, the parables of the sower (here with the explanation), the net, the true scribe, the workers in the vineyard, the two different sons, and the unjust servant are not in other gospels. Some aspects of Jesus' life on earth not found elsewhere in the Bible include Christ's ancestry traced to Abraham, the praise of the children in the temple, the suicide of Judas, Pilate's wife and hand-washing, the opening of the tombs, and the Great Commission given to the disciples in Galilee.

The Importance of Studying Matthew

Christians have found the Gospel of Matthew great reading for their personal growth and for sharing with children of all ages the story of God's love for us in Christ. The study of Matthew is important for teens who are learning to make their faith their own. Adolescents seek independence in many areas of their lives. Their faith is pushing for independence, too, and Matthew's gospel provides useful teaching for such growth. An understanding of the message and meaning of God's Word in this book will be a solid foundation on which teens can build as they seek to be Christ's disciples and act out His love for them in service and worship.

A Note for Class Leaders

It would serve you well to have a *Concordia Self-Study Bible* or a comparable tool available to you as you lead these lessons. The commentary introducing the gospel and in the text can be invaluable if you are not familiar with it. Also, the *LifeLight* study of Matthew (two parts, 18 lessons available from CPH) can provide in-depth material for reference.

Plan Ahead

Take some time now to read each lesson's objectives and lesson outline. Make a list of items needed for each study. Especially note the need for your students to know their date of Baptism for lesson 4. Lesson 3 has an optional opening activity that uses a video camera to record interviews with people. You probably want to have the students do this before that lesson begins rather than using class time. It can be done either during the week or before your class begins that day. Something for the students to write with, Bibles (preferably the New International Version), and copies of Student Pages are needed each week.

Lesson Structure

Each lesson has three parts. They are *Getting Acquainted with the Lesson, Getting Acquainted with Scripture*, and *The Empowered Self in Action*. The first part introduces the lesson to the students through activities designed to get them focused on the theme of the study. The second part gets them into the Bible passages applicable to the lesson's objectives. And the last part allows the students to apply the lesson to their lives.

A Few Suggestions for Your Study

1. Use a variety of learning styles. Remember, everyone learns differently. Most teens learn best through experience. With that in mind, various activities are used to introduce the lesson themes.

2. The lesson plans offer some options. Each lesson contains more material than you will need. This gives you the opportunity to select activities that fit your group. Be sensitive to the needs of the young people in your class. Listen to them and respond to their needs.

3. Active learning fits the needs of contemporary youth. Young people live in a fast-paced world. Limit any activity to 15 minutes. Allow discussions to flow freely. Encourage participants to express their feelings as well as their thoughts.

4. Relax and have fun. If the young people see you putting yourself into the lesson, they will follow along. Be yourself. Talk about your faith struggles. By sharing your feelings you will give students permission to share theirs.

5. Invite the young people to bring their own Bibles and to record insights about the text.

6. Occasionally, you may want everyone to use the same version of

the Bible. This will help the group focus on the lesson without becoming lost in the different translations and interpretations.

7. Several times students will be asked to read aloud a section of Scripture. In those situations, ask for volunteers. However, if you must select someone, choose a capable and confident student. Never use reading the Bible as a punishment for misbehavior in class.

8. After a Bible reading, check to make sure all the students understand important words and phrases. Taking time to clarify concepts will make your class more meaningful for your students.

9. When you ask the class to complete an exercise within a given time, be sure to give a two- and then a one-minute warning before you call the class back to order.

10. If your group is larger than eight, consider working in two or more groups when the lesson calls for discussion or personal sharing.

11. Model the behaviors, the confidentiality, and the vulnerability you expect from your class. You have the position and opportunity to increase the spiritual depth of your discussion by your actions. Protect the person who risks sharing from the heart, and encourage your students to give their full attention to the words of their peers.

Building Relationships

Jesus desires to be our close friend as we take our daily walk of discipleship. It is beneficial to have Christian friends who can support us in that journey. Hopefully, this class will enable some of those relationships to develop. It begins with you.

Take time to get to know the members of your class. The most important time in any session is the 10–15 minutes before class begins. You need to be prepared to teach prior to that time. Be ready to greet the students as they arrive. Listen with interest as they talk about the things going on in their lives.

Try to spend some time outside of class with your students. Eating together is a great relationship-builder. Call them on the telephone just to talk. Remember their birthdays and recognize each special achievement with a card or note.

Strive to build relationships within the class as well. Encourage small-group discussions. Be sensitive to those who might be left on the outside. Attempt to help the others understand their situation in the hope that they will seek to include them. Do your best to promote class unity.

Teacher/Student Relationships

Our teaching may only be as strong as our relationships with our class members. As we learn to know our students—and as they learn to know us—our ability to direct our teaching to their lives and their ability to listen both improve.

Some suggestions:

- Maintain a balance between being the teacher and being a friend. You're not a teenager. And you don't need to be one or act like one to relate to your class. Your are, however, a potentially significant person in the lives of your students. Many young people seek adults with whom they can relate and on whom they can count.

- *Don't talk down to your students.* High school students see themselves as "no longer children." They will relate best to adults who give them credit for all their strengths and potential, and who are gentle with reminders that they have some areas in their lives in which they need to grow. Resist sarcasm, teasing, and put-downs of any kind.
- *Participate with your students* in class activities. Share your own responses as examples to the students. If you ask students to cut, paste, or draw, be a willing participant in the activity. It will quickly blunt any perception that such activities are childish.
- *Sit, if possible.* With a small group, in a single circle, or around a table, sit at the same level as your class. Stand when leading several small groups or in a situation where all the participants may not be able to see you otherwise.
- *Refrain from "teacher only" privileges.* If food or drink is not allowed for the students, finish yours before you enter the room or save it until after class. If refreshments are appropriate, make sure they are available to the entire class.

If your group is small, you may be able to participate in one of the small-group discussions during class. If more than two or three groups form, it may be wiser to "float" among the groups. Recognize that young people may filter their responses and opinions with an adult present in their small group.

Be sensitive to the feelings of your students. As you respect them, they will grow in their respect for you.

(From *Bible Impact, Book 4*, page 73, © 1994 CPH. All rights reserved.)

Teaching without Student Pages

In response to the requests of many teachers, the Bible Insights studies are designed with Student Pages that you may duplicate. However, your class may be getting tired of a steady diet of study sheets, or perhaps you or your students simply don't like them. You may wish to omit some and use others. Or you may wish to do without them entirely. Here are some suggestions for adapting the lessons:

- Write response activities (sentence completions, multiple-choice questions, or true/false statements) on the chalkboard or newsprint before class. Students can still respond and discuss in small groups or as a whole class.
- Write Bible references and discussion questions on index cards. Distribute the cards to individual students or small groups at the appropriate time.
- Adapt Student Page activities so they can be done without the sheet of paper. For example, rather than having the students mark a set of response scales on a Student Page, have them stand at imaginary points along the longest wall of your classroom. The wall becomes the scale as you read the response statements.

- You can frequently lead a class discussion from questions on the Student Page or invite small groups to discuss the questions one at a time.
- For some activities, you can have the students respond on blank paper or draw their own version of the Student Page illustration before completing the activity.
- Omit activities that are strictly paper-oriented and substitute more active ones. Even teenagers enjoy simple games and *active* learning assignments.
- If no other solution is obvious, scan the Student Page activity to determine the purpose it serves in the progression of the lesson and summarize that point directly. Or invent another method of communicating it to the students.

Evaluation

Evaluation should be a part of every session. Take time after each session to reflect on activities that went well or didn't work and why, concepts some students didn't grasp, and new issues or concerns you heard from your students.

Occasionally, take time after class to discuss with at least a few of the students the following questions: What was the best part of the class session today? If you were the teacher, what things would you do differently? What is the most important thing that you learned?

Incorporate the things you learn into your future lesson planning.

A Teacher with Authority 1
(Matthew 5–7)

Focus

In Jesus' day as now, people were looking for a teacher with authority to teach the truth of God's Word. Jesus was just such a teacher sent by God the Father. Yet He and the Father are one God. Jesus' teaching is God's Word. Only He has the authority to teach us the will and ways of God. These teachings provide us with direction and truth as the Holy Spirit creates faith in Christ as the Messiah, the One who rescues us from sin.

By the power of the Holy Spirit, we are able to recognize the authority of Jesus, teaching us to hear and apply His Word to our lives, and to respond with commitment, worship, and service.

Objectives

That by the power of the Holy Spirit the participants will

1. identify the source of Jesus' teaching authority;
2. summarize Jesus' message in the Sermon on the Mount;
3. grow in their willingness to study Christ's teachings and apply them in their lives.

Materials Needed

- Copies of Student Pages 1–4 for each student
- Pencils or pens
- Bibles
- Marker board or newsprint and markers

Lesson Outline: A Teacher with Authority

Activity	Minutes	Materials Needed
Warmup	10	Symbols or pictures of authority, copies of Student Page 1, pencils or pens
The Sermon on the Mount	30	Copies of Student Page 2 or 3, Bibles, pencils
Wise and Foolish Builders	10	Copies of Student Page 4, Bibles, pencils
Closing	5	

Preparation

Review the options for teaching described in the leaders material and choose those that will best meet your needs and the needs of your students. Make sufficient copies of the Student Pages you will need for your regular students and a few extra for visitors. Also gather other materials you may need such as pictures or symbols of authority for the "Powerful People" activity.

Warmup

Powerful People

Bring two or three pictures or symbols of authority. Some symbols might include a toy police car or badge, a referee's shirt or whistle, a traffic sign, or a flag of your state, province, or country. Pictures of a teacher, an umpire, a government official the students would recognize, or other people in positions of authority would work also.

Use Student Page 1 to introduce the idea that authority is not something to fear, distrust, or shun. Many times people in authority provide us with help, direction, or support. Have the students read over the list of people who may have authority over their lives. Ask if any authorities are missing from the list. Direct the students to add them.

Now have the students mark the six people on the list who have the most power over them. This is purely a personal ranking with no right or wrong answers. Take some time to discuss this activity. If your class is larger than five, break into groups of three or four by any means you wish. With five or fewer students you may lead the class through this activity yourself. Have each person share his or her responses within the small groups. Ask each group to list the three most powerful authorities that they agree upon. When they have completed this task, discuss the following questions with the whole group.

1. Name your group's three most powerful authorities. Where do these people get their authority? Why do they have power over you? (Answers will vary.)

2. Where would Jesus rank on your list? Explain why you would place Him higher or lower than others. (Again answers will vary. This is not the time to challenge student responses. The issue of Jesus' authority will be discussed in the heart of the lesson.)

3. How does authority in general make you feel? (Accept their answers.)

4. What makes you respect some authorities more than others? (Power of the authority, respect for them, or consequences for disobedience.)

5. Why do you allow certain people to have authority over you? (Answers to question 4 will apply. In addition, some students may point out that we anticipate benefits from people in authority or that we are taught to respect authority automatically.)

6. Where does Jesus' authority comes from? (He and God the Father

are one God. All the authority, wisdom, and power of the triune God is His according to His divine nature.)

Allow your students to be honest with their answers. Do not evaluate their comments or let others argue about their points. After touching on each of the questions above, move directly into the next section.

The Sermon on the Mount

Select one of the following activities.

What Did Jesus Say?

In the Sermon on the Mount, Jesus teaches from the Old Testament, with which the listeners are probably very familiar. Yet He desires that they know the Scriptures in a new and more relevant way. He expands the people's understanding of the Word of God.

To get the students started, distribute copies of Student Page 2. Have the students find **Matthew 5–7** in their Bibles and direct them to complete the Student Page according to the instructions. You might have them work in pairs, or use the groups they were in during the previous activity as work teams.

Have the groups share the topics they have marked as unfamiliar. (Answers will vary.) Ask, "Were your surprised by any of the topics Jesus taught about?" Review the unfamiliar passages or pick three or four topics that you think your students will find most interesting. Use the following questions to discuss them.

1. What was the common practice of the Jews in this area? (Use cross-references or a Bible commentary to locate relevant passages from the first five books of the Bible, the Jewish Torah. A few of the topics are summarized on Student Page 3.)

2. How did Jesus reinterpret the issue? (Look for the words *But I say to you.* They signal Jesus' teachings.)

3. Does Jesus make it easier or harder to live "according to the Law"? (Answers may vary. Often Jesus' teaching is more "strict." He is showing that it is pointless to rely on our own strength to keep the Law and please God. We all sin and fall short of God's expectations. We need a Savior to win forgiveness for us and to help us live according to God's will. Occasionally, Jesus' way may seem easier—for example, praying and giving gifts privately. Point out that, even without *public* accountability, we are still accountable to God for our actions.)

Summarize this activity by pointing out that Jesus as God's Son was truly God and had the authority to interpret God's Word. He also gives us forgiveness for our failure to abide by God's Word and helps us live according to God's will. Also point to the wide variety of things Jesus taught. He seems to have something to say about every area of our lives.

Or …

The Sermon on the Mount Roleplay

Try an alternate approach to this material if you have a class that is active and likes to move around. Have the students study the scene in **Matthew 5–7.** Pick a student to be Jesus, others to be His disciples, and let the rest be the crowd. Set Jesus on a chair or table with the rest on the floor. Select two or more of the topics from Student Page 2, and, as time allows, have Jesus "teach" the crowd using the Bible as a basic script. You could have some members of the class act out the teachings as Jesus is talking. Choose topics that involve people interacting with each other.

Or ...

Jesus Teaches with Authority

As an alternate or supplementary activity, use Student Page 3. Follow the instructions on the page. You may lead the entire class through the page or have them work on their own or in small groups. They should read each passage you assign and write in the space provided the new meaning Jesus applied. (Look for the words *But I tell you.* Jesus' new meaning will follow.) The teaching can be summarized in a few words or a short phrase.

For example in **Matthew 5:31–32,** Jesus places additional restrictions on when men could divorce their wives.

Wise and Foolish Builders

This part of the lesson will help the students take home the thought that Jesus has authority to teach them also. God desires to be at work in each of us by the power of His Word and Spirit. We will study the last few verses of chapter 7 to help the students apply Christ's words to their lives and understand His authority over them.

Hand out copies of Student Page 4. Have someone in the class read **Matthew 7:24–29.** Then ask each question and have the students answer orally. They should also be encouraged to write answers on their papers.

To help you lead the students through this, here are some possible responses:

1. Answers will vary.
2. Hearing and practicing His teachings.
3. Teachings from others, or not practicing the teachings of Jesus.
4. Because some people saw Jesus as an ordinary teacher, not as the Son of God. They expected Him to teach like the other rabbis, scribes, and religious leaders—not with divine authority.
5. Jesus was sent by the Father. He fully knew His Father's Word and will. Where many human teachers would only quote other teachers, Jesus revealed the heart of the eternal God. He Himself was true God.
6. Remember what Jesus taught, and pray the Holy Spirit will give you strength and encouragement to follow those teachings.

Closing

You or a class member can lead a closing prayer. Ask God to continue to teach you this week and to give you strength to accept His authority and to do His will. Pray that the Holy Spirit will lead you and give you the power Jesus promised to follow His teachings.

Extending the Lesson

If you have additional time or need to redirect the students because attention is drifting, challenge them to find the parallels that are present between the familiar beginning of Jesus' Sermon on the Mount, the Beatitudes ("declarations of blessing"), **Matthew 5:1–12**, and the Ten Commandments. Ask the students to volunteer each of the Commandments in order (see **Exodus 20:1–17**). Some possible responses are as follows:

You shall have no other gods.	**Matthew 5:5,** "Blessed the meek" (that is, those who acknowledge the authority of others).
You shall remember the Sabbath day.	**Matthew 5:6,** "Blessed are those who hunger and thirst after righteousness."
You shall not kill.	**Matthew 5:7,** "Blessed are the merciful."
You shall not commit adultery.	**Matthew 5:8,** "Blessed are the pure in heart."

Your students will find others.

Powerful People

____ Policeman

____ Teacher

____ Parent

____ Older brother

____ The President
     or Prime Minister

____ Employer

____ Store clerk

____ Grandmother

____ Pastor

____ Younger sister

____ Best friend

____ Other _____

____ Other _____

Matthew, Student Page 1

What Did Jesus Say?

Scan **Matthew 5–7** in your Bible. See if you can summarize Jesus' teaching on each topics in a few words. Mark topics that are new to you with an exclamation point [!]. Mark topics about which you have questions with a question mark [?].

Matthew 5
___ The Beatitudes
___ Salt and Light
___ The Fulfillment
of the Law
___ Murder
___ Adultery
___ Divorce
___ Oaths
___ An Eye for an Eye
___ Love for Enemies

Matthew 6
___ Giving to the Needy
___ Prayer
___ Fasting
___ Treasures in Heaven
___ Do Not Worry

Matthew 7
___ Judging Others
___ Ask, Seek, Knock
___ The Narrow
and Wide Gates
___ A Tree and Its Fruit
___ The Wise and Foolish
Builders

Jesus Teaches with Authority

Jesus taught the Word of God in a way the people had not heard before!
Read these passages from Matthew's gospel and the former teaching understood by the people of God. Then fill in the "New Meaning" column with your
understanding of what Jesus says we are to be and to do.

Scripture and Former Teaching	New Meaning
5:21–22: Do not murder or call your friend a name of contempt	
5:27–28: Do not commit adultery	
5:33–37: Do not break an oath	
5:38–42: Paybacks are all right	
5:43–48: Hating your enemy is all right	
6:1–4: Gifts are given publicly	
6:5–6: People pray publicly	
6:19–21: Treasures on earth	
7:1–5: Judging others is all right	

The bottom line is ...

According to **Matthew 7:12,** what is a one-sentence summary of the Law and the Prophets?

Wise and Foolish Builders

Read **Matthew 7:24–29**

1. What kind of "storms" do you expect in your life?

2. What is the rock that Jesus is recommending as a strong foundation for your faith?

3. What is the sand?

4. Why were the crowds amazed?

5. The crowds had probably heard many other teachers. What was different about Jesus?

6. What do you need in your life this week to survive any storms you might experience?

A Healer with Power 2
(Matthew 8–9)

Focus

In Jesus' day, people flocked to a healer with real power to heal their ills. Young people live in a world in which they encounter evil, sickness, and pain. They, too, need healing. God sent His Son, Jesus, into our world to restore our broken bodies and souls. Throughout His earthly ministry, Jesus plundered Satan's kingdom, healed the sick and demon-possessed, and forgave those tormented by sin. In Christ, we have a Messiah with power. Through faith in Him, we share in the forgiveness of sins and Christ's healing power.

Objectives

That by the power of the Holy Spirit the participants will
1. identify influences of Satan in their world;
2. see Christ's healing power at work;
3. rejoice in Christ's forgiveness and healing power in their lives.

Materials Needed

- Copies of Student Pages 5–8 for each student
- Pencils or pens
- Bibles
- Marker board or newsprint and markers
- Band-Aids
- Video camera or cassette recorder (optional)

Lesson Outline: A Healer with Power

Activity	Minutes	Materials Needed
Warmup	15	Band-Aids, Bibles, Student Page 5, pencils or pens, marker board or newsprint and markers
We Need a Healer with Power	15	Student Page 6, Bibles, pencils
Thank You, Jesus	10	Bibles, Student Page 7
Who Answers God's Mail?	15	Bibles, Student Page 8, pencils, video camera or cassette recorder (optional)
Closing	5	

Preparation

Review the leaders material and decide whether you will use the "Extending the Lesson" activities or other alternatives that are offered. Gather the supplies needed for the activities you choose and make sufficient copies of the appropriate Student Pages.

Warmup

Whom Do You Call?

In this section of the lesson the students will begin to identify the influence of Satan and sin in their lives. They will also begin to see how God helps them deal with Satan and his evil plans. Distribute copies of Student Page 5 to the students. The Student Page is in two parts. On the top half, ask the students to think about and describe the people they rely on in their lives for help, comfort, and advice. Have them fill the space behind each problem with a name of a resource person they can expect to help with that kind of problem.

Provide a Band-Aid or other brand of adhesive strip for each person, the bigger the better. Have the students apply the strips to the places they hurt most at the moment, pointing out physical, emotional, or spiritual pains they have. Ask them to explain their placement of the strips and what hurt they are covering.

If you don't have any Band-Aids, or as an alternate activity, you could ask if anyone has a physical scar he or she can show or an emotional scar he or she can tell to the group. Encourage the students to share other stories about their injuries, illnesses, or major disappointments in life.

Continue this activity by discussing the following questions with the students. (A suggested procedure or possible student responses follow each question.)

1. What needs can Jesus take care of in our lives? (Direct the students to the bottom of the Student Page. Ask the students to write down some of the needs they think Jesus can take care of in their lives. Invite volunteers to share and write their responses on newsprint or a marker board.)

2. Where do the evils of sickness, emotional distress, disabilities, death, and the like come from? (Help the students to recognize that some of these problems are the result of sin or Satan's influence in the world. Since the fall of Adam and Eve in the Garden, all of creation and all of God's creatures have suffered the effects of the curse of sin. Not all such distress is the *direct* result of sin, however. It is evident that God uses negative circumstances to work His will in our lives—such as Jonah's three-day imprisonment in the great fish.)

3. Can He take care of *all* of our physical, emotional, and spiritual needs? (Or ask, "What physical, emotional, and spiritual problems do you have that Jesus is *not* able to help with?") Refer them to **Matthew 9:2–8** if they want or need a hint. This passage assures us that Jesus is able to address all our troubles.

4. Why can we go to Him? (To identify why He is able to help, point out that Jesus is the Son of God sent to save us from our sin. He died on the cross to make that happen and now dwells in us through faith to strengthen, calm, and heal us according to God's will.)

Extending the lesson. Have the students use **Matthew 9:2–8** and information from the discussion to produce a commercial which would advertise "Jesus Christ, M.D." as the one who is there all the time to take care of whatever ails a person. It could be made for either radio or television. Make sure the students include these elements: (1) when Jesus is ready to help (on call 24 hours a day, seven days a week), (2) the kinds of problems He can help with, and (3) why He can be of service. The students could tape their commercials with a cassette recorder or video camera, or present them "live" to the class.

We Need a Healer with Power

People needed a Messiah to provide a solution for the problem of separation from God. In sending Jesus Christ to earth as a human being, God provided for us a healer with power. To illustrate that, Matthew gives example after example of people healed by Jesus. Distribute Student Page 6 and direct the class to review **Matthew 8–9.** Working individually, with a partner, or in small groups, students should first list the symptom or source of sin of the person in the space provided. This may be an illness, situation they were in, possession by demons, or need for forgiveness. These are all consequences of sin. Each is addressed by Jesus the Messiah through the power He has as the Son of God.

After listing the symptoms from Matthew's examples, tell the students to write in their own name on the last blank. Have them list for themselves at least one symptom, result, and/or source of sin in their lives. This may be something they are worried about, behavior they feel is sinful, a physical problem they have, or anything in their life that needs to be corrected or resolved.

Extending the lesson. If your class enjoys drama, invite them to roleplay scenes from **Matthew 8–9.** You or a "quick study" could portray Jesus. Have other students be the leper, Centurion, paralyzed man, dead girl, sick women, or blind man (choose two or three as time allows). Use the Bible verses for your script, ad lib as you desire, and then ask each character, "How do you feel now that Jesus has healed you?" Make sure you get an answer to that question!

Thank You, Jesus

Distribute copies of Student Page 7. The students are to pick one person from **Matthew 8–9** for whom they would be willing to write a thank-You note to Jesus. Use the sheet of stationery illustrated on the top of the paper to do this. Tell the students to express the feelings this person must have had as he or she realized what Jesus did for him or her. Have the students sign the name (it could be fictitious) or designation (the man you healed, a grateful mother) of the person for whom they are writing.

23

Then have them write their own thank-You notes to Jesus. Tell them to use this time to express their gratitude to Christ for the physical, emotional, and spiritual healing He has given them in their lives, and to especially thank Jesus for the forgiveness He provided for them.

Who Answers God's Mail?

This section of Scripture becomes real for us as we recognize opportunities to respond to the needs of people around us. We may be given the opportunity to assure someone of the forgiveness God provides or to meet a physical or emotional need. **Matthew 9:35–38** reveals that we have many such opportunities to serve others in Jesus' name. God enables those whom He has called to faith through His Word to reflect His grace to others. What a privilege!

Pass out copies of Student Page 8. Ask someone in the class read the Bible passage, then discuss the questions.

1. Have the students list all the people they know who could use the healing presence of Christ right now. Focus on people in their world they can name, not a general "poor people, the sick," etc.

2. Help the students realize that God is calling on Christians everywhere to be His representatives, ambassadors, and workers in His harvest fields. This means your students are the people God wants to use to meet the needs of the people named.

3. How do they go about meeting those needs? Spend some time brainstorming solutions, listing things that could be done by individuals or the whole class, and praying about God motivating you to serve Him by working to meet the needs brought up in class. Encourage and plan activities that can be done, maybe that afternoon, to begin bringing Christ to people in your world. Do not be afraid to invite the students to really do the activities that they see are possible and be ready to hold them, and yourself, accountable. Ask the students to be ready next session to report the experiences they had in serving Christ through serving others.

Closing

Invite students to name specific people or kinds of people that have come to their minds during the class session to be included in the closing prayer. If they are willing, invite them to speak a sentence prayer for those they name. Begin the prayer time with thanksgiving to God for His gift of forgiveness and healing through Jesus Christ. Include a petition for forgiveness for the times when we fail to live and love others according to His will. Incorporate the prayer concerns of the class. Close with a petition for God's continued work in the lives of His people both to desire and to do acts of service for others.

As an alternate approach to the closing prayer, invite volunteers to share their personal thank-You notes to Jesus (bottom of Student Page 7) as parts of the prayer.

For Next Week

If you can plan ahead and wish to the use the "man on the street" interviews suggested in warmup activity 4 next week in study 3, assign a team of students to do these with people from the community or your congregation.

Whom Do You Call?

When stuff happens in your life, to whom do you go for help, comfort, or advice?

I wonder if God still likes me?

To whom would you turn when you …

have the flu? _____

have a lawsuit filed against you? _____

have a disagreement with a teacher? _____

are in a car accident? _____

are betrayed by a friend? _____

break a leg? _____

suffer from a guilty conscience? _____

feel like a failure? _____

have disobeyed God? _____

Matthew, Student Page 5

We Need a Healer with Power!

"He took up our infirmities and carried our diseases." **Matthew 8:17, Isaiah 53:4**

A Person in Need	Source/Symptom of Sin	The Solution
Man **(8:1–3)**	_____	A Messiah!
Centurion **(8:5–13)**	_____	A Messiah!
Peter's mother-in-law **(8:14–15)**	_____	A Messiah!
Disciples **(8:23–27)**	_____	A Messiah!
Two Men **(8:28–34)**	_____	A Messiah!
Man **(9:2–8)**	_____	A Messiah!
Girl **(9:18–19, 23–26)**	_____	A Messiah!
Woman **(9:20–22)**	_____	A Messiah!
Two Men **(9:27–31)**	_____	A Messiah!
Man **(9:32–34)**	_____	A Messiah!
_____ (Put your name here)	_____	A Messiah!

"Which is easier: to say, 'Your sins are forgiven,' or to say, 'Get up and walk'? But so that you may know that the Son of Man has authority on earth to forgive sins …" Then He said to the paralytic, "Get up, take your mat and go home." … They [the crowd] were filled with awe; and they praised God, who had given such authority to men." **Matthew 9:5–8**

Matthew, Student Page 6

Thank You, Jesus!

Dear Jesus,

Love,

Dear Jesus,

Love,

Who Answers God's Mail?

"When He saw the crowds, He had compassion on them, because they were harassed and helpless, like sheep without a shepherd. Then He said to His disciples, 'The harvest is plentiful but the workers are few. Ask the Lord of the harvest, therefore, to send out workers into His harvest field.'" **Matthew 9:36–38**

1. Who among the people you know needs Jesus' healing right now?

2. Whom might God use to respond to the needs of people?

3. How do they (we!) do that?

We Do!

An Answer to the Big Question

(Matthew 16:13–20)

Focus

All who hear the Good News of Jesus Christ today are ultimately challenged to respond to the "big question," the one Jesus asked of His disciples: "Who do *you* say that I am?" Christian faith begins in the Spirit-guided recognition that Jesus Christ is our Savior, sent by God to pay the penalty for our sin and rescue us from death and hell. In His death and resurrection, Jesus brings us back to our loving heavenly Father and a new relationship rooted in His love and forgiveness.

Objectives

That by the power of the Holy Spirit the participants will
1. confess Jesus Christ as the Son of God;
2. celebrate Christ as their Messiah and King;
3. share with others the Good News that Christ is the Son of God.

Materials Needed

- Copies of Student Pages 9–12 for each student
- Pencils or pens
- Bibles
- Marker board or newsprint and markers
- Bag of candy
- Video camera, VCR, and television (or a tape recorder)
- A high-quality pen or marker for writing on paper
- Poster board (optional)

Lesson Outline: An Answer to the Big Question

Activity	Minutes	Materials Needed
Warmup	15	Student Page 9; marker board or newsprint and markers; bag of candy; video camera, VCR, and television (or tape recorder); poster board (optional)
The Big Question and the Answer	20	Bibles, Student Page 10
My Declaration	10	Bibles, Student Page 11, pencils, a high-quality pen or marker for writing on paper
Closing	5	

Preparation

Take time before you teach this study to reflect on your own faith—your answer to Jesus' question, "Who do you say that I am?" Use the background information that follows and other resources as needed. Also review the study and identify the activities you will include in your lesson and the materials you will need. Especially, plan ahead if you wish to include the "man on the street" interviews suggested in warmup activity 4.

Background

Throughout time many have asked questions about the tremendous influence Jesus Christ has had on the world. Other great teachers and personalities have come and gone in history. Why have they not had as big an impact as Christ? Who is this man from Nazareth, anyway?

Some have tried to understand Jesus simply as a great teacher—only one among many. Jesus ranks "up there" with the masters: Buddha, Confucius, Mohammed, and other wise men and women who taught about God, the world, and our human condition. The story of Jesus' life and teaching is merely another reference work to consult when figuring out the meaning of life.

Others look at His miracles and say Jesus was a great magician or sorcerer. They insist that Jesus learned the hidden secrets of nature or tapped into the mysterious powers of the human mind and body in order to heal people. Rejected by His own people, Christ worked outside the boundaries of Jewish tradition and writings. Therefore, Christ would have experienced or learned something more than what was available to the rabbis of the time. This made Him attractive to certain people who followed Him.

Many have struggled with the idea that God would take a human form. They say this reduces the power or awesomeness of the Supreme Being. Therefore, Christ must have been just a man, but one who became so great in His understanding that He seemed like or perhaps actually became a god.

The witness of the Bible shatters all these mistaken views. We see that even as Jesus walked the dirt roads of Israel, people were asking who He really was. The four Gospels testify that Jesus is the Christ, the incarnate Son of God, one with God the Father, yet truly man. This lesson will help teens understand and proclaim the truth of Scripture as the Holy Spirit works through the Gospel to create and strengthen their faith.

Warmup

Select one or two of the following activities.

1. Hang a piece of poster board, newsprint, or other large piece of paper on the wall near the entrance to your class. If the board is near the entrance it could be used. Write on the top, "Who is Jesus?" As the students enter, ask them to write a word or phrase to answer that question.

2. Play a word-association game. Tell a student a word and have him

or her say the first thing that comes to mind. Have each student do it at least once. Use words related to religions of the world. Suggestions: *Buddha, New Age, pyramids, Savior, wizard, Koran, Hindu, Bible, sorcerer, Jesus, Satanism, channeling, ghost, seance, Jewish, Mormon, crystals, guru, mantra, prophet, Great Spirit, miracle,* and *witches.*

3. Use any of the words above and play a picture-guessing game. Divide into two teams. Have a person from one team come forward. Give them a word and have them draw it on newsprint, large paper, or a marker board. Have their team guess what it is. If they cannot get it within 30 seconds or so, let the other team make a guess. If neither guesses it, share the answer and have a person from the other team try the next word. Keep rotating contestants between teams. Award points and consider a small reward for the team who has the highest total at the end, such as a bag of candy large enough to be shared with the other team also.

4. Do "man on the street" interviews, asking various people in your congregation or from the community, "Who do you think Jesus is?" Record these brief encounters with a video camera or tape recorder. You could assign students to do this during the week before class or the morning before class begins. (Do not use class time for this. It could take the whole hour!) Play the tape to the class. Ask the students if they agree with everything they heard.

Or ...

5. Set up a video camera in class and ask the students to answer the question as they arrive. Play the video back so that all can see and enjoy it. Affirm the students' efforts and comment about how difficult it can be to answer tough questions "on the spot."

No matter which option you use, have fun with it. Then hand out Student Page 9 and put the students to work in groups of three. Ask each group to agree on a list of responses they think their friends would have to the question, "Who is Jesus?" They must all agree before they can check that response on the Student Page. Give them about three minutes to do this. Then ask for a report to the whole group of the responses they feel their friends would have.

The Big Question and the Answer

Distribute copies of Student Page 10. Read or have a volunteer read, **Matthew 16:13–20.** These few verses portray Jesus' identity. The reality and power of His identity—"You are the Christ, the Son of the living God"—are clearly stated. And the future of Christ's church is also revealed.

Then direct your students to work through the questions. After allowing a few minutes for their work, invite volunteers to share their responses. Use the following information to expand their responses.

1. The disciples shared four responses people gave about Jesus' identity—John the Baptist, Elijah, Jeremiah, another prophet **(verse 14).**

2. Peter stated the truth that Jesus was the Christ, the Son of the living God **(verse 16).**

3. Jesus said this was revealed to Peter by the Father (verse 17).

4. In our lives God has sent the Holy Spirit to reveal to us the truth about Christ. We understand who Jesus is because in our Baptism and by the power of the Word the Holy Spirit has brought us to faith.

5. Verse 18 points out the promise Jesus has made to His church: nothing, not even hell, will overcome it.

6. Your students may have struggled with the "So what?" question. The reality is that our confession of Jesus Christ as the Messiah, the Savior sent by God, has life-changing consequences. These will be more fully discussed in the session 4, but students may have mentioned things such as: living in hope, salvation, new life, having a spiritual purpose, or being reconciled with God. As you discuss this point, direct the students to another confession Peter makes on behalf of the disciples in **John 6:66–69.**

My Declaration

Use Student Page 11 to help students take this lesson home. You may want to copy this page on heavier paper of a pale color for a real "certificate" look.

Distribute copies of Student Page 11 and direct the students to write an affirmation of faith, or a statement of their belief. Have each person finish the five sentences with statements that reveal their beliefs about Jesus. These could include His being the Son of God, Healer, Forgiver, One who died for their sins, sacrificial Lamb, Provider of salvation, Savior, and other statements that show what work Christ did for God's chosen people.

When they are completed, have the students date and sign their statements. Then have them exchange pages with another student and sign each others' as witnesses.

Or …

Challenge the class to create a motto they can live by in the coming weeks. Divide students into groups of three. Ask each group to come up with a list of three suggestions for the class motto based on what they have said in their personal creeds. Have them present these to the class. Then have the whole class vote on one they would like to use. You may want to do a "straw poll" first, and narrow the list down to two or three selections. Then have the class take a final vote by show of hands or ballot.

When a motto has been chosen, you, or a student with good printing skills, should write it on poster board or a large sheet of paper. Have each student also create a personal copy on blank paper. Post the class copy where it can be seen easily by all in the room.

Suggest to the students that their affirmation of faith and the class motto can serve as daily reminders of what Christ means to them. Encourage them to display it prominently at home.

Closing

Consider closing this session with a hymn of faith or a contemporary Christian song such as "Our God Is an Awesome God" as a further affirmation of faith. Then lead the students in a prayer of thanks for their Spirit-given faith and for continued faithfulness by God's grace to their Lord and Savior, Jesus Christ.

Extending the Lesson

The Ecumenical Creeds—the Apostles' Creed, the Nicene Creed, and the Athanasian Creed—are the responses of the whole church to the question *Who is God?* These creeds were written and adopted by councils representing the entire church. The Apostles' Creed in its present form is from the eighth century; it was based on a much earlier creed, the Old Roman Creed from the third century. The Nicene Creed was drafted at the Councils of Nicaea and Constantinople in the fourth century. The Athanasian Creed, named for but perhaps not written by the fourth-century church father Athanasius, may have been written in the fifth or sixth century.

While the entire texts of the creeds are in a sense a reaction to questions about the nature of the Son and Spirit and their relationships to God the Father, the second article of each speak directly to the issue of this session, "Who do you say Jesus Christ is?" Student Page 12 provides the texts of the two most widely used of the three ecumenical creeds. Invite the students to study these texts, choose phrases that are descriptive of the Son, and respond to the question, "What specific information or new insight does this phrase provide to our understanding of who Jesus is?" Some of the phrases and possible responses follow. Many others responses are possible.

- **only son:** Jesus is God's Son and shares a one-of-a-kind relationship with the heavenly Father **(John 3:16).**
- **begotten of the Father before all ages:** Begotten means "brought forth." The church has used this phrase to convey that Jesus was not "made" by God nor born in a normal human way, but was, is, and will be eternally God **(John 1:1–2).**
- **being of one substance with the Father:** To counter charges that Jesus was another god, separate from God the Father, or not truly divine, the Nicene Council determined to use this phrase, declaring that Jesus and God the Father share the same essence and are indeed one God.

Who Do You Say Jesus Is?

If you were to ask 10 friends tomorrow, what would they say? Check all of the responses your group agrees would be heard from the people you know.

A Jewish rabbi

The Savior of the world

A religious fanatic

A man who became god

The Great Spirit

A swear word

A great teacher

The Son of God

A mystery

A wizard

One of many gods

Just a man

Matthew, Student Page 9

The Question and the Answer!

When Jesus came to the region of Caesarea Philippi, He asked His disciples, "Who do people say the Son of Man is?" They replied, "Some say John the Baptist; others say Elijah; and still others, Jeremiah or one of the prophets." "But what about you?" He asked. "Who do you say I am?" Simon Peter answered, "You are the Christ, the Son of the living God." Jesus replied, "Blessed are you, Simon son of Jonah, for this was not revealed to you by man, but by My Father in heaven. And I tell you that you are Peter, and on this rock I will build My church and the gates of Hades will not overcome it. I will give you the keys of the kingdom of heaven; whatever you bind on earth will be bound in heaven, and whatever you loose on earth will be loosed in heaven." Then He warned His disciples not to tell anyone that He was the Christ. (Matthew 16:13–20)

1. According to the disciples, what were people saying about Jesus?

2. What was Peter's response?

3. Who revealed this to Peter?

4. Who reveals to us who Jesus is?

5. What does Jesus say about His church?

6. So what?

My Declaration

I hereby declare the following statements to be an accurate portrayal of my faith. Thanks be to the Holy Spirit for revealing the true Christ to the world!

I believe ...

I believe ...

I believe ...

I believe ...

I believe ...

I believe ...

Signed this _____ day of _____, A.D._____

Witnessed by _____

Sealed by Baptism for eternity

The Ecumenical Creeds

The Apostles' Creed

I believe in God, the Father almighty, maker of heaven and earth:

And in Jesus Christ, his only son, our Lord: who was conceived by the Holy Spirit, born of the virgin Mary, suffered under Pontius Pilate, was crucified, dead, and buried: he descended into hell, the third day he rose from the dead, he ascended into heaven, and is seated on the right hand of God, the Father almighty, whence he shall come to judge the living and the dead.

I believe in the Holy Spirit, the holy Christian church, the communion of saints, the forgiveness of sins, the resurrection of the body, and the life everlasting. Amen.

The Nicene Creed

I believe in one God, the Father almighty, maker of heaven and earth and of all things visible and invisible.

And in one Lord Jesus Christ, the only-begotten Son of God, begotten of the Father before all ages, God of God, Light of Light, very God of very God, begotten not made: being of one substance with the Father, through whom all things were made: who for us men and for our salvation came down from heaven, was incarnate by the Holy Spirit of the virgin Mary, and was made man: who for us, too, was crucified under Pontius Pilate, suffered, and was buried: the third day he rose according to the Scriptures, ascended into heaven, and is seated on the right hand of the Father: he shall come again with glory to judge the living and the dead, and his kingdom shall have no end.

And in the Holy Spirit, the Lord and giver of life, who proceeds from the Father and the Son: who together with the Father and the Son is worshiped and glorified; who spoke by the prophets.

And I believe one holy, Christian, and apostolic church.

I acknowledge one Baptism for the remission of sins, and I look for the resurrection of the dead and the life of the age to come. Amen.

The Apostles' and Nicene Creeds are reprinted from THE BOOK OF CONCORD, edited by Theodore G. Tappert, copyright © 1959 Fortress Press. Used by permission of Augsburg Fortress.

A New Life **4**
(Matthew 28)

Focus

Jesus came to seek those who were lost, dead in sin, to rescue and renew them. His obedience to the Father led Him to die on the cross to atone for our sin. This payment for our sin provided us with something we could get nowhere else—a new life! The old is gone and has been replaced by God's gifts of forgiveness and salvation.

We all need Christ's new life. Some of us were baptized as infants and received the washing of regeneration. Others may have come to faith as the Holy Spirit worked through a sermon or a friend's witness about Jesus. In either case, the new life in Christ is a gift of the Spirit, the beginning of a lifelong pattern of daily repentance, forgiveness, and renewal—all through the work of Christ.

Objectives

That by the power of the Holy Spirit the participants will
1. contrast life with and without Christ;
2. recognize sources of fear and acknowledge that the resurrection overcomes fear;
3. celebrate the resurrection in their lives.

Materials Needed

- Copies of Student Pages 13–16 for each student
- Pencils or pens
- Marker board or newsprint and markers
- Party decorations and refreshment (optional)
- Hymnals (optional)
- Squirt guns (optional)

Lesson Outline: A New Life

Activity	Minutes	Materials Needed
Warmup	20	Copies of Student Page 13, pencils or pens, party decorations, food and beverages, squirt guns (optional)
A New Life in Baptism	20	Bibles, copies of Student Pages 14 and 15
I Can't ... or I Won't	15	Bibles, copies of Student Page 16, pencils, hymnals (optional)
Closing	5	

Preparation

Review the activities in this lesson and choose, adapt, and prepare those that will best suit your teaching style and the needs of your students. In particular, you may wish to provide resources for a celebration of new life (see "Warmup"). Make sufficient copies of the Student Pages you will use for class members and visitors.

Warmup

Celebration of New Life

A key element of this lesson is the celebration of new life through our Baptism and the promised resurrection. To enrich this celebration, you may wish to decorate your class area for a party. Your students might enjoy helping. Ask them to bring treats, appetizers, and beverages. Set out the food before class begins. As people come have them fill a plate and glass to enjoy.

Strive to know dates of Baptism for everyone in your class. Ask the students the week before or call them sometime before class. On a calendar, write each person's name on the date he or she was baptized. Explain to the class that their baptismal dates are more important than their birth dates because Baptism marks the beginning of their new life in Christ. This is why you are having a party!

If you are the adventurous sort and do not mind a little mess, buy a few cheap squirt guns and play some water games with your students. Shoot at a target drawn on a paper plate. See who can fill a small cup the most with one squirt of water from the gun. Blow up balloons and see who can make them move the fastest across the room. Be ready for someone to shoot at another person in the room. This may be the signal that it is time to move on to the next activity. All of this is designed to emphasize the point that we can celebrate our Baptisms.

Celebrity Switch-a-Roo!

Hand out copies of Student Page 13. Ask the students to mark the appropriate box indicating their willingness to change places with each type of celebrity. Have them share their choices with the whole group. Randomly ask why they chose to switch or not. Make sure the students share what it is they like about the lifestyle of any celebrities with whom they would switch places.

A New Life in Baptism

There are several key points to fully understanding **Matthew 28.** One is to appreciate the meaning of being baptized into the name of God. Student Page 14 is designed to introduce this truth to your class. Some may never have heard or thought about it. The awesomeness of receiving God's name through Baptism is sometimes not recognized. Even in their confirmation the students may not have understood the fullness of what they were proclaiming.

Hand out copies of Student Page 14. Read, or have a volunteer read, the introductory material on the top of the page. Discuss the three questions with the class. Or divide the students into small groups and direct them to discuss the questions and report to the whole class. After about five minutes, invite each group to respond to one of the questions. The following will assist you in leading the discussion.

1. Answers may vary. Ask the students to be honest and open with their answers.

2 In Baptism, Christians receive the blessings of a heavenly Father, the benefits of Jesus' death on the cross (victory over sin, death, and Satan), and new life and power through the Holy Spirit dwelling in them. At Baptism every Christian receives these things in their fullness: the forgiveness of sins, rescue from death and Satan's power, and eternal salvation.

3. As we remember our Baptism into Christ, God moves our hearts to be convicted of our sin, leads us to repentance, and through forgiveness makes us pure and holy. He does this for and in us daily. The Holy Spirit helps, comforts, and sustains us, because nothing can separate us from the love He has for us in Christ **(Romans 8).**

Now hand out copies of Student Page 15. Have students take turns reading one verse from **Matthew 28:16–20.** Discuss the questions on the page as a class or in small groups with reports to the whole class. Responses to the questions should include the following.

1. Usually this comment is meant to say that a person does not have enough fun or pleasure in his or her life. It may mean he or she needs a purpose for what he or she is doing, or needs to find something productive to do.

2. Answers with vary. Encourage the students to share how Jesus' presence and power helps them in making decisions, finishing projects, etc.

3. The students' dreams may be anything they want to do or accomplish in their lifetime. The effect of the Great Commission on those dreams is that God may be calling them to act out their faith in a way they had not considered or wanted.

4. Paul wants us to know the hope we have in Christ, the riches of our inheritance, and the power God has given us. The church is Christ's body, the fullness of Him who fills everything and heads everything for us.

5. Have the students think about their needs and opportunities at the moment. This is a personal matter, so let the students share as they feel comfortable. This would be a good opportunity to remind them of the forgiveness and strength available to them in the Word and the Sacraments. Connected with Christ, students can witness and serve in His power and authority.

Extending the Lesson

Consider asking one or two people to come and share with your class how God has used or changed them. Maybe a missionary is available to speak, or an adult who has changed careers to be involved full-time with some work of the church. Perhaps a part-time worker in a food pantry, a short-term mission trip participant, or anyone involved in any sort of congregational ministry can share their experiences. Ask your pastor for suggestions. It may be a real treat for your students to hear your guest's story and to see that God puts "real people" to work in His kingdom.

I Can't ... or I Won't

The ideal outcome of this lesson will be for the new life Christ promises to be more evident in the students' lives. The Holy Spirit is working in them through the Word shared in class. Now provide time for the students to think about what they can do with the help of Christ. The passage on the bottom of Student Page 16 is too great a promise to ignore.

Hand out copies of Student Page 16 and ask the students to mark each line to indicate their feelings about the fear or the confidence they have in being able to carry out the work indicated. Then have them share this information in small groups. Allow about a minute for each student to tell their group where they stand in their estimate of themselves.

Then work with the entire class to come up with a list of 10 activities they could get involved with in the congregation. Encourage them to commit themselves to follow through on one or more of the items they list.

Extending the Lesson

As an option, you might want to provide your class with a time of confession for their failure to appreciate what Christ has done in their lives. You might want to use an order of confession from your congregation's hymnal. See if your pastor is available to lead this worship time. He might also be able to speak about the call he has to serve in the church and your congregation.

Closing

Invite your students to spend a little time in reflection on their Student Pages and the opportunities God provides for their new life in Christ to be extended to others. Then lead a time of prayer. Your students may be comfortable in speaking one-sentence prayers asking God's help in reflecting His love to others or giving thanks for His work in their lives. Begin and end the prayer yourself.

You may wish to use Psalm 51, speaking it responsively verse by verse. You could alternate leader and group, males and females, etc.

Celebrity Switch-a-Roo!

Have you ever wanted to be someone else? Now is your chance! For each person listed below, mark the appropriate box indicating your willingness to switch lifestyles for the next six months.

	No Way	Maybe	Sure	Definitely
Major league baseball player				
Rock music star				
Governor				
Movie star				
Country music singer				
Winner of a $20 million lottery				
Football quarterback				
Olympic gold medal winner				
President or Prime Minister				
Talk-show host				

In the Name of ... God!

Matthew 28:19 says we are to baptize "in the name of the Father and of the Son and of the Holy Spirit." Read the following explanation of what that phrase means.

In Judaism this phrase indicated that a person was being effectually committed to something or someone. One circumcised "in the name of the covenant" was committed to the covenant, brought under its blessing, and placed under its obligations. A person baptized "in the name of the Father" has God as his gracious Father. Baptized in the name "of the Son," one receives all the benefits of the Son's redeeming act. Baptized in the name "of the Holy Spirit," one receives the life-giving, life-sustaining power and presence of the Holy Spirit.

(From the *Concordia Self-Study Bible.* Copyright 1986 by Concordia Publishing House. All rights reserved.)

1. What happened at your Baptism? What does it mean to you to be baptized "in the name of the Father and of the Son and of the Holy Spirit?"

2. What are the daily blessings of Baptism?

3. How does God support, help, comfort, and sustain you today because of your Baptism?

Get a Life!

Christ is Life is Christ is Life is Christ is Life

Read **Matthew 28:16–20.**

1. "Get a life!" your friends say. What do they mean?

2. Jesus says we "get a life" through our Baptism into His death and resurrection. In what ways are Jesus' resurrection promises real for you today?

3. What dreams do you have for your life? How does the Great Commission affect your dreams?

4. Look up and read **Ephesians 1:18–23.** What does Paul want us to know? How does he describe the church?

5. In Baptism, we received all we need to live the new life in Christ. What are the opportunities before you to witness to your new life?

I Can't ... or I Won't

Place an *X* on each line indicating how fearful or confident you are about participating in the activity.

When I think about...

worshiping regularly
I am **FEARFUL** /———/—-/—-/—-/—-/—-/—-/—-/ I am **confident**

attending Bible study
I am **FEARFUL** /———/—-/—-/—-/—-/—-/—-/—-/ I am **confident**

going to youth group
I am **FEARFUL** /———/—-/—-/—-/—-/—-/—-/—-/ I am **confident**

ushering for a worship service
I am **FEARFUL** /———/—-/—-/—-/—-/—-/—-/—-/ I am **confident**

helping to lead a youth Sunday worship service
I am **FEARFUL** /———/—-/—-/—-/—-/—-/—-/—-/ I am **confident**

attending a church youth retreat
I am **FEARFUL** /———/—-/—-/—-/—-/—-/—-/—-/ I am **confident**

going on a servant event or mission trip
I am **FEARFUL** /———/—-/—-/—-/—-/—-/—-/—-/ I am **confident**

becoming a full-time missionary
I am **FEARFUL** /———/—-/—-/—-/—-/—-/—-/—-/ I am **confident**

telling a non-Christian friend that Jesus rose from the dead
I am **FEARFUL** /———/—-/—-/—-/—-/—-/—-/—-/ I am **confident**

sharing my faith with someone I have never met
I am **FEARFUL** /———/—-/—-/—-/—-/—-/—-/—-/ I am **confident**

What other activities are possible in the church for us to do?

Which activities do you think God could be leading you to be involved with?

I can do all things through Him who gives me strength. Philippians 4:13